ROLLING WITH THE PUNCHES

Monica Boeh

PAGE PUBLISHING, INC.
Conneaut Lake, PA

First originally published by Page Publishing 2021

ISBN 978-1-6624-2047-4 (hc)
ISBN 978-1-6624-2048-1 (digital)

Printed in the United States of America

I would like to dedicate this story to all children who live with a disability. You empower others by your daily strength to not let your struggles define you. Be like Rebel.

1

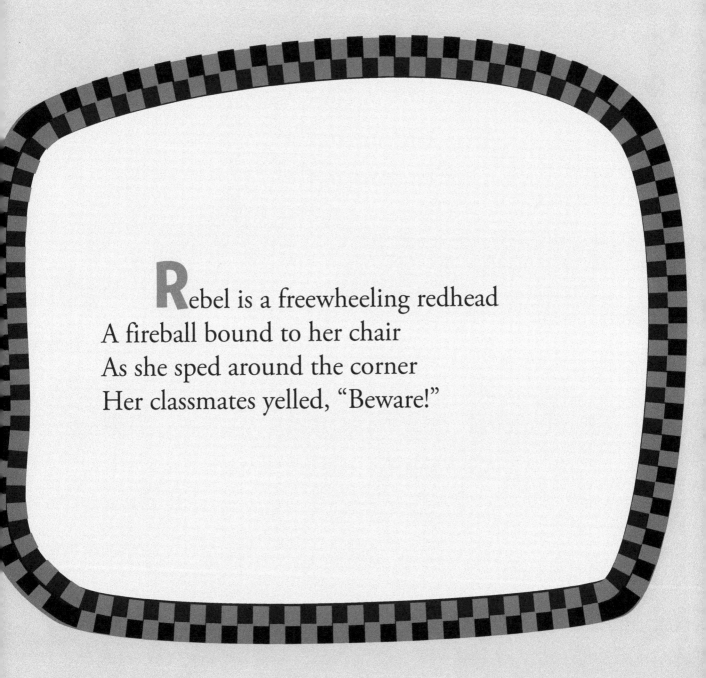

Rebel is a freewheeling redhead
A fireball bound to her chair
As she sped around the corner
Her classmates yelled, "Beware!"

She never let her disability stop her
And she never gave in to her woes
For she lived one day at a time
While avoiding other people's toes.

Rebel lived for speed
Never dreading a potential crash
Fearless as nothing stopped her
Even when she got whiplash.

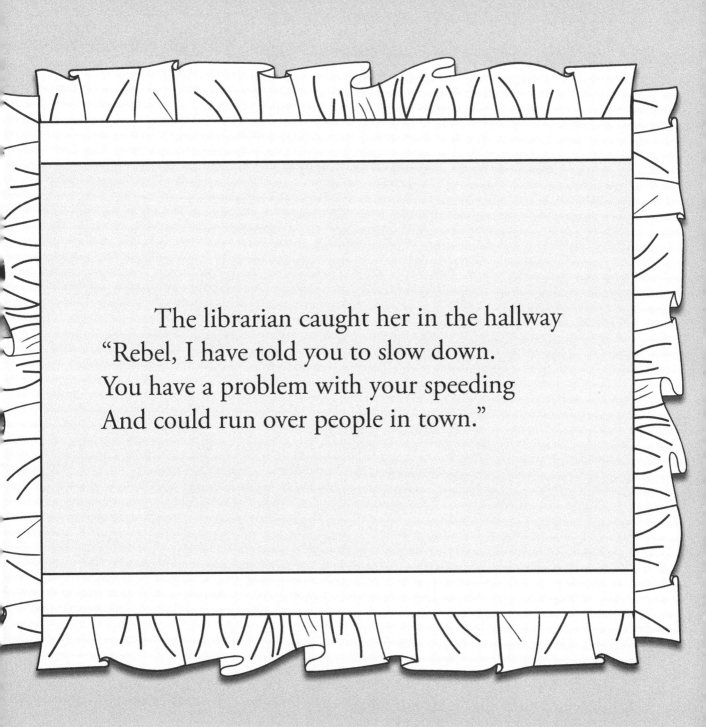

The librarian caught her in the hallway
"Rebel, I have told you to slow down.
You have a problem with your speeding
And could run over people in town."

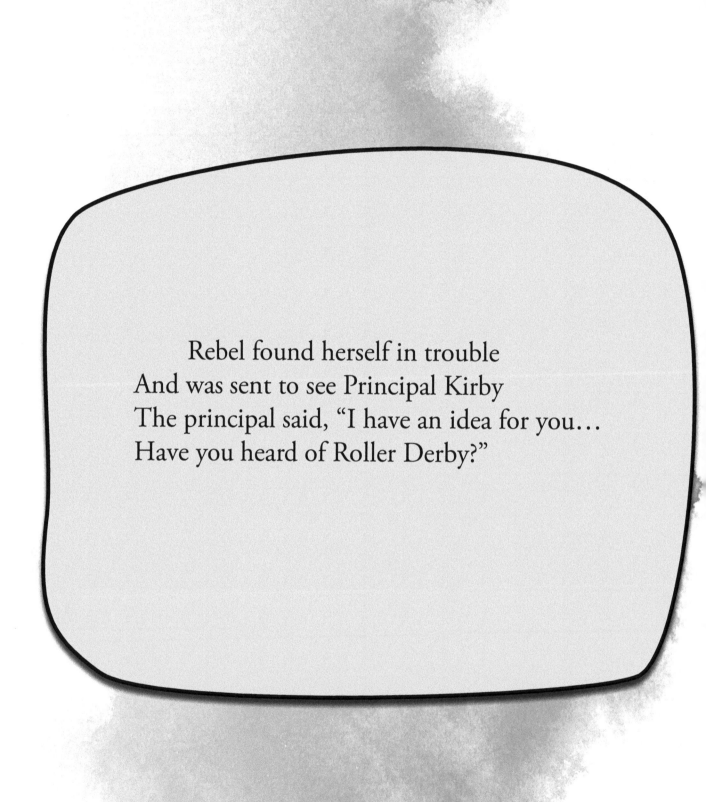

Rebel found herself in trouble
And was sent to see Principal Kirby
The principal said, "I have an idea for you…
Have you heard of Roller Derby?"

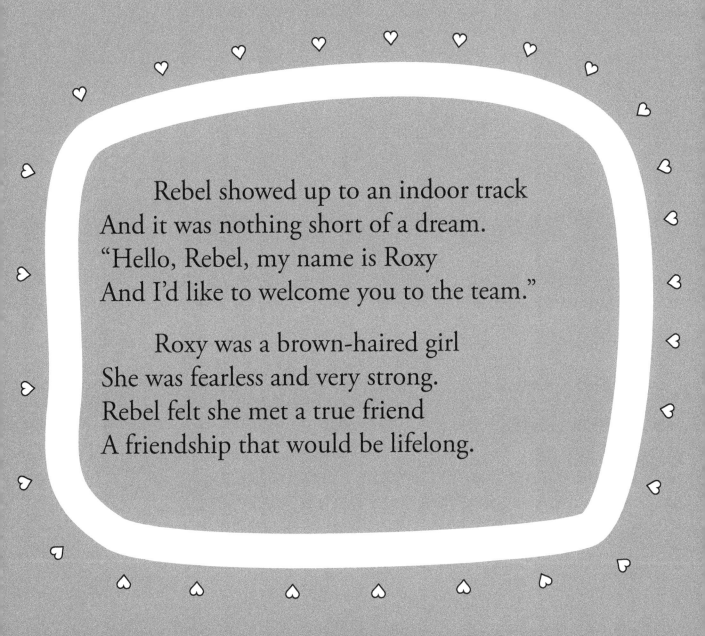

Rebel showed up to an indoor track
And it was nothing short of a dream.
"Hello, Rebel, my name is Roxy
And I'd like to welcome you to the team."

Roxy was a brown-haired girl
She was fearless and very strong.
Rebel felt she met a true friend
A friendship that would be lifelong.

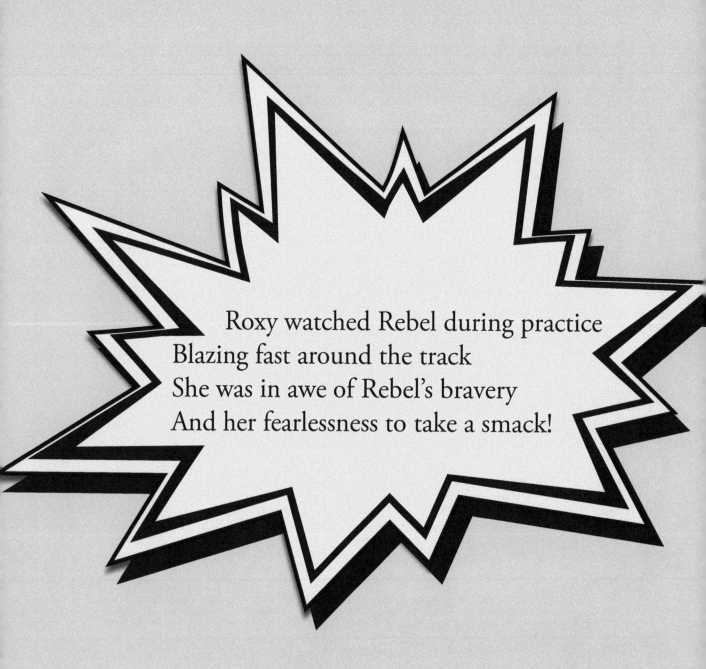

Roxy watched Rebel during practice
Blazing fast around the track
She was in awe of Rebel's bravery
And her fearlessness to take a smack!

Rebel was finally ready to race.
Owning the track in all her glamour
Rebel was ready to win for her team
And was now a roller derby jammer.

Round and round the track she went
Rebel rolling with lightning-fast speed.
She was so focused on winning,
She kept thinking, "Two points is all we need."

But then Rebel suddenly lost focus
When an opponent's elbow smashed into her face
Causing her wheelchair to spiral out of control
And she took a nasty fall from grace.

16

The fans remained silent.
Then the audience shouted, "Oh dear!"
Shock spread across the track
But Rebel was determined to persevere.

There was fire in Rebel's eyes
And the fall didn't affect her one bit.
She put her helmet on very tightly
To protect her from a future hit.

Rebel wheeled at full speed
With enough momentum to fly high
She flew over all of her opponents
To win and break the tie.

Rebel's teammates gathered around her
Cheering loudly that they won the game.
Her teammates raised her up above their heads
And the whole crowd chanted her name.

Rebel realized that being in a wheelchair
Was a great thing after all.
She found her strengths and her talents
And the importance of getting back up
when you fall.

About the Author

Monica Boeh is a resident of Saint Joseph, Missouri, where she lives with a physical disability. She works at a nonprofit, independent living center where she helps people overcome their own obstacles.

CPSIA information can be obtained
at www.ICGtesting.com
Printed in the USA
BVHW021220190821
614777BV00006B/515